SCAT OMNIBOOK

For B♭ Instruments • Transcribed Exactly from the Original Recordings

Transcribed by Mark Johnson

ISBN 978-1-4803-5563-7

HAL•LEONARD®
CORPORATION
7777 W. BLUEMOUND RD. P.O. BOX 13819 MILWAUKEE, WI 53213

Visit Hal Leonard Online at
www.halleonard.com

THE HISTORY OF SCAT

Scat singing is a form of jazz vocal improvisation that does not use words. Instead, the vocalist either uses nonsense syllables or imitates musical instruments.

Scat singing has its true beginnings with the 1926 Louis Armstrong recording of "Heebie Jeebies." As the story goes, during the recording session for the song, Armstrong's music fell onto the floor. To keep the recording going, he started improvising his own gibberish words over the chorus of the song, assuming it was a ruined take. After all was said and done, it was that take of "Hebbie Jeebies" that was kept, and a new genre was born.

Artists at the time who picked up on the scat trend included Cab Calloway and Duke Ellington, whose "Creole Love Call" featured Adelaide Hall doing a vocal impression of a muted trumpet. Soon, other artists joined in on the vocal craze, including Dizzy Gillespie, Eddie Jefferson, Mel Torme, Sarah Vaughan, and a true master of the craft, Ella Fitzgerald.

It was while she was singing with Dizzy Gillespie's big band that Ella Fitzgerald started playing around with her vocals. Instead of singing lyrics, she imitated what the horns were doing. Her performance on the 1945 recording of "Flying Home" with the Vic Schoen Orchestra set a new standard for scat, much as Louis Armstrong's "Heebie Jeebies" had done years earlier.

The songs in this volume include selections by many of the classic jazz scat artists, including Ella Fitzgerald, Sarah Vaughan, Mel Tormé, and Eddie Jefferson, along with more contemporary vocalists, such as Karrin Allyson, Ann Hampton Callaway, and Roberta Gambarini.

You'll find these helpful features in this "omni" volume:
- 71 note-for-note transcriptions
- Meticulous easy-to-read notation
- Recording reference included with the song title
- No lyrics are included for the scat solos, as the spelling of syllables are too varied and numerous
- Any B♭ instrumentalist can use this book. The solos lend themselves to those wanting to learn the style and expand their improvising prowess.

Enjoy!

CONTENTS

Air Mail Special

from *Ella Fitzgerald: Gold – Verve 951102*

Music by Benny Goodman, Jimmy Mundy and Charlie Christian

This is the name of

this song; it's called The Air Mail Spe - cial. Get on,

Scat

get on the spe - cial car - go air - mail!

All Blues

from *Ernestine Anderson: Blues, Dues and Love News – Quest 9362-45900-2*

By Miles Davis

Sea, _____ the sky, _____

shades, _____ all _____ hues, _____ all _____ blues, _____ all blues. _____

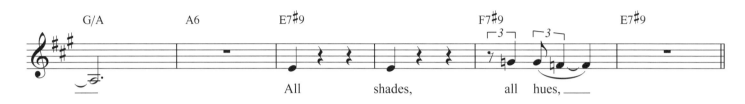

All shades, all hues, _____

oh, _____

_____ all blues.

All _____ blues. _____

All blues. _____ All blues. _____

_____ All _____ blues. _____

All God's Chillun Got Rhythm

from *Mel Tormé: It's Easy to Remember – Recall 258*

Lyrics by Gus Kahn

Music by Bronislaw Kaper and Walter Jurmann

trou - bles __ don't ___ mean a thing. _____

When they start __ to go "sha - ba - doo - be - doh dum," all your trou - bles go

'way, hey! _ All God's chil - lun got __ swing.

Scat

Yeah, all ____ God's chil-

- lun got swing. ___

Scat

Hey hey, ___

hey hey, ___ hey hey, ___ all God's chil-lun got ___

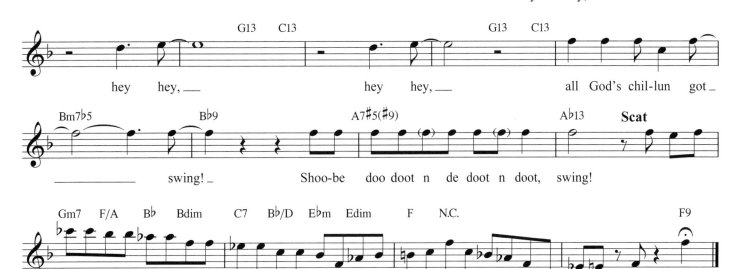
_____ swing! ___ Shoo-be doo doot n de doot n doot, swing!

Yeah!

All of Me

from *Ella Fitzgerald: Ella Swings Gently with Nelson – Verve 5193482*

Words and Music by Seymour Simons and Gerald Marks

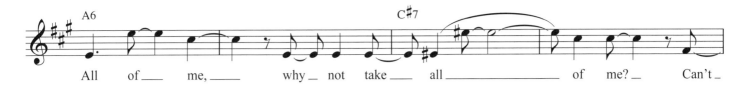

All of ___ me, ___ why __ not take ___ all _____ of me? _ Can't _

___ you __ see, ___ I'm no ___ good _____ with - out you.

Take my lips; _____ I _____ want ____ to __ lose ___ them. _ Take _

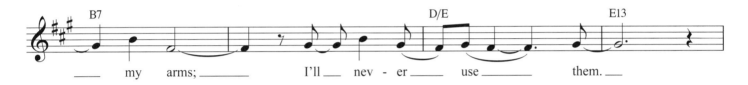

___ my arms; _____ I'll __ nev - er ____ use _____ them. _

Your good - bye _____ left me with eyes _____ that _____ cry. ___ How _

___ can _ I ____ go on ___ dear _____ with - out ___ you? ___

You _____ took _____ the part ____ that once _____ was __ my heart, _ so why _

___ not take ___ all _____ of me? _____

Scat

19

Come _ on _ and _ take, _____ take _ all _ of _ me. _____

Freely
Scat

All of Me

from *Sarah Vaughan: The Essential – Verve 512904*

Words and Music by Seymour Simons and Gerald Marks

Scat

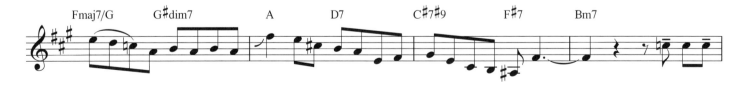

Bernie's Tune

from *Tierney Sutton: Unsung Heroes – Telarc 83477*

Words by Mike Stoller and Jerry Leiber
Music by Bernie Miller

Of - fice clerks, so - da jerks picked it up so soon; _____

mil - lion-aires, e - ven squares hum-min' Ber-nie's Tune. _____

% **Scat**

Chords 2nd x: C6/G   Am7/G   Dm7/G   G7♭9   C6/G   Am7/G

Dm7/G   G7♭9   C6/G   Am7/G   Dm7/G   G7♭9

Both times: C6/9

To Coda ⊕

Fluglehorn Solo
2

Billie's Bounce
(Bill's Bounce)
from *Ella Fitzgerald: Bluella – Pablo 2310960*
By Charlie Parker

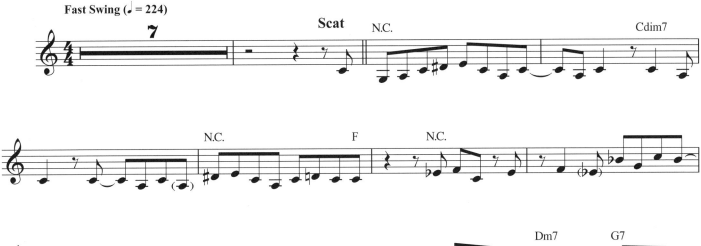

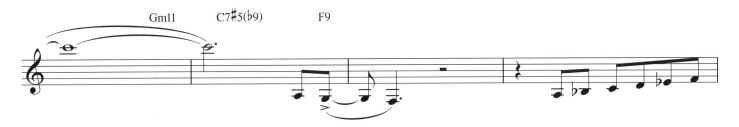

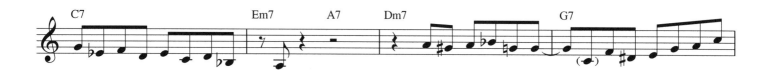

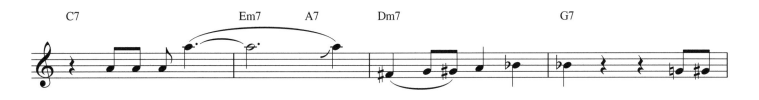

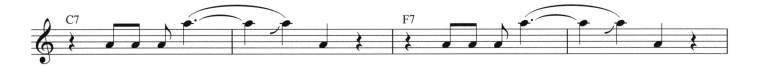

A real dumb guy, and I love him just the same. ___

Bli Blip

from *Ella Fitzgerald Sings the Duke Ellington Songbook – Verve VE2-2535*

By Duke Ellington and Sid Kuller

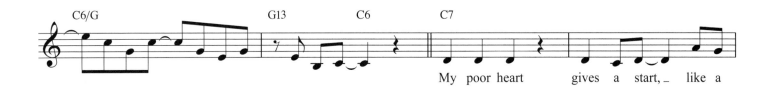

My poor heart gives a start, _ like a

jit - ter - bug, just won't stop. So mix your croon - ing _____ with _

_ my spoon-ing, and let me blow _ my top. My! Your

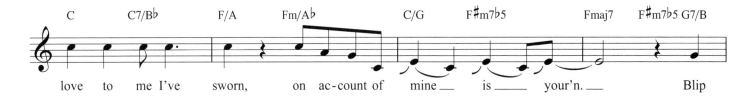

love to me I've sworn, on ac-count of mine _ is _____ your'n. _ Blip

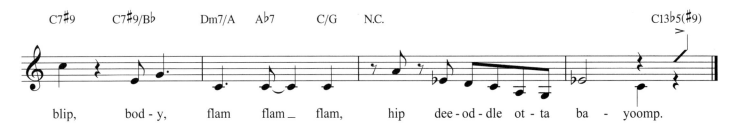

blip, bod - y, flam flam _ flam, hip dee - od - dle ot - ta ba - yoomp.

Blue Lou

from *Ella Fitzgerald: The Legendary Decca Recordings – GRP 648*

Words and Music by Irving Mills and Edgar Sampson

Un - til she dis - cov - er her lov - er,_____ she'll al - ways be Miss Blue._____

Scat

Ooh, ooh, ooh, Lou, ooh,__

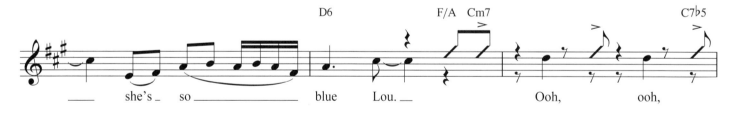

_____ she's __ so _____ blue Lou. __ Ooh, ooh,

Scat

blue Lou. Oh,_____ blue ___ Lou. _

Blue _____ Lou. __ Her ba - by was such a pho -

-ny; he left her blue and lone - ly. ____

Blue, ____ blue, __ blue, ____ blue, ____ true, ____ true, __ true, __

____ true. ____ So ____ Blue went __ bro - ken - heart - ed

be - fore her ro - mance got start - ed. ___ Cry - ing, sigh -

- ing ___ is all she ev - er do. ___ For - get - ting, __ re -

- gret - ting ___ the love she nev - er knew. ___ So ___ she's ___

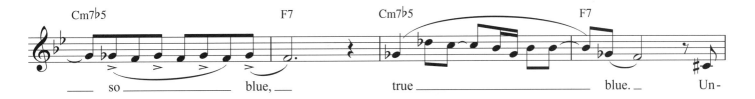

____ so ____ blue, ____ true ____ blue. _ Un-

til she dis - cov - er her lov - er, ____ she'll al - ways be ___ Miss Blue. ___

She just wants love, pret - ty ba - by; ___ true ____ blue ____ Lou.

Blue Skies

from *Ella Fitzgerald Sings the Irving Berlin Songbook – Verve 5438302*

Words and Music by Irving Berlin

No-tic-ing the days hur - ry-ing by; when __ you're in love, my, how they fly. __

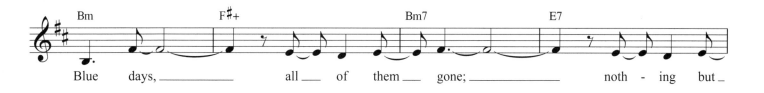

Blue days, _____ all __ of them __ gone; _____ noth - ing but __

__ blue ___ skies ___ from now __ on. _____

Scat

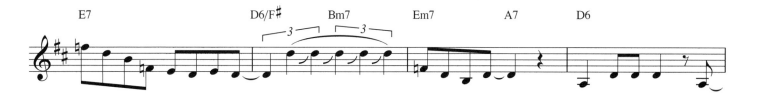

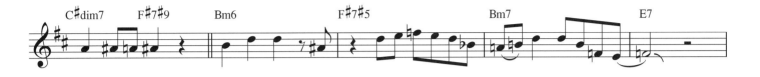

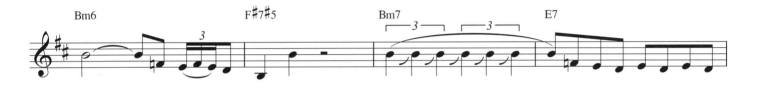

I

never saw the sun shin - ing so bright; nev - er saw things go - ing oh so right. __

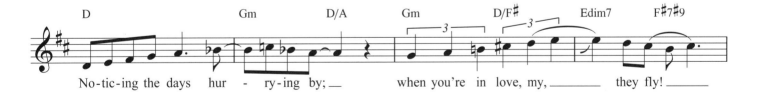

No-tic-ing the days hur - ry-ing by; __ when you're in love, my, _____ they fly! _____

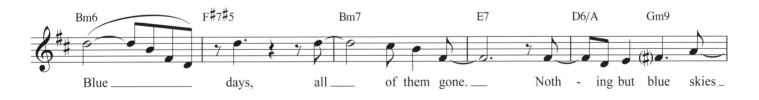

Blue _____ days, all ___ of them gone. __ Noth - ing but blue skies __

____ from __ now __ on.

Bluesette

from *Ann Hampton Callaway: Easy Living – Shanachie Records 5126*

Words by Norman Gimbel
Music by Jean Thielemans

Scat

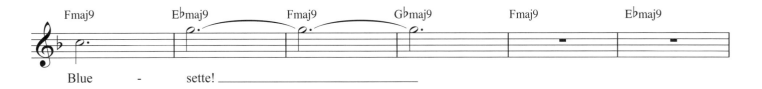

Blue - sette! _____

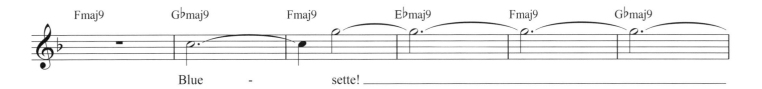

Blue - sette! _____

_____ Blue - sette! _____

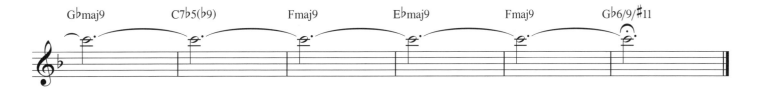

_____

Bluesette

from *Ella Fitzgerald: Sophisticated Lady – Pablo 5310*

Words by Norman Gimbel
Music by Jean Thielemans

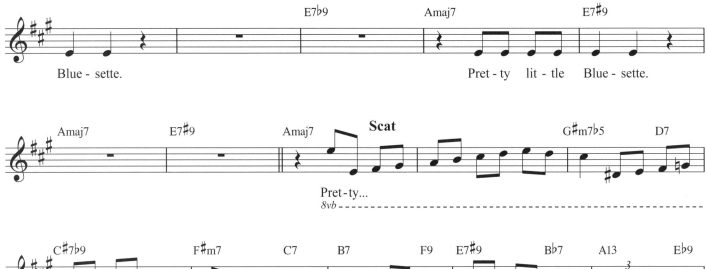

Blue - sette.   Pret - ty   lit - tle   Blue - sette.

Pret - ty...

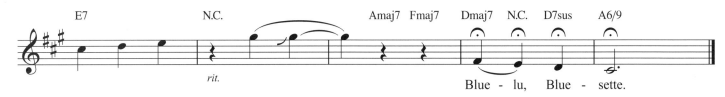

Blue - lu,   Blue - sette.

Centerpiece

from *Roberta Gambarini: Easy to Love — Now Forward Music Inc. 1122*

Music by Harry "Sweets" Edison

Words by Jon Hendricks

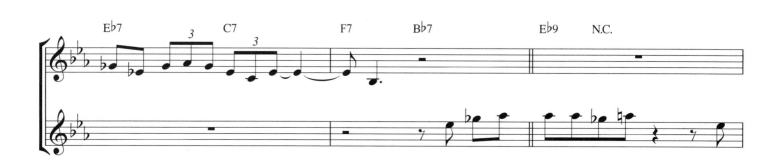

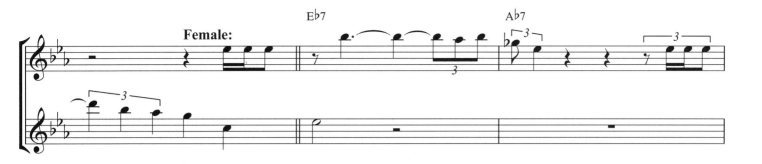

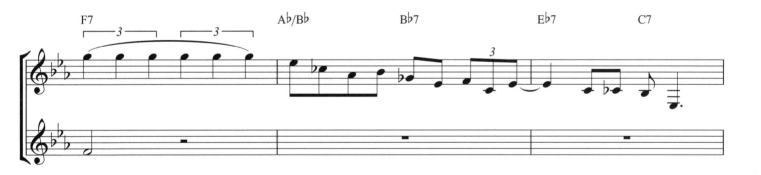

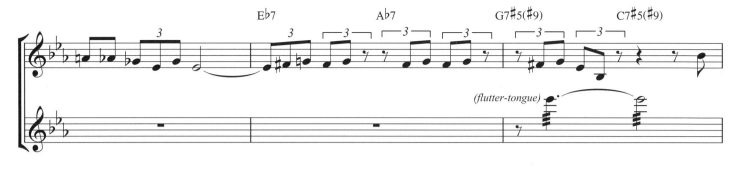

Yeah, _____ ev-'ry day, ev-'ry day, _ I have the blues. _

_____ Ev - er - y day, ev - 'ry day, ev - 'ry day,

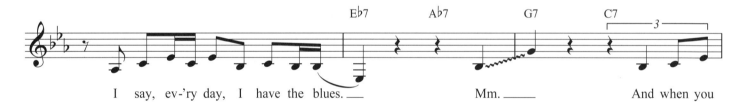

I say, ev-'ry day, I have the blues. __ Mm. ____ And when you

see me wor-ry, ba - by, it's 'cause, it's you _ I hate to ____ lose. __

_____ No - bod - y loves me; no - bod - y seems to care.

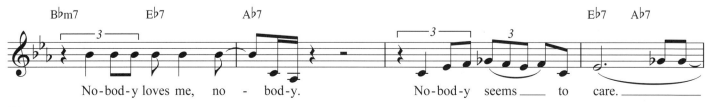

No-bod-y loves me, no - bod-y. No-bod-y seems ___ to care. ___

Speak-in' a-bout bad luck and trou-bles, you know, you know I've had my share. But, the more I'm with you, pret-ty ba-by, the more I feel my love in-crease. I'm build-ing all my dreams a-round you; our hap-pi-ness will nev-er cease. 'Cause noth-in's an-y good with-out you, and...

Scat:

Male:

Female:

Body and Soul

from *Eddie Jefferson: Body and Soul – OJC 396*

Words by Edward Heyman, Robert Sour and Frank Eyton
Music by John Green

He was twen-ty years a-head of time, and he knew it, but he kept right on a-cook-in'. He went

all a-round the world mak-in' rhy-thm, 'cause mu-sic sure was in him, and I know it was.

Ben - ny Good - man was King of Swing, ev - 'ry -

bod - y loved to dance; Haw - kins knew he had a chance of play - ing

mu - sic, so he blew. And he blew, and he blew, and he blew; he blew his ten - or.

And he played it sum-mer and win-ter. Then he cut his mas-ter-piece, and I'm try'ng to sing it for you.

Hope that I am get-ting through to ev-'ry-one; there I go. I did-n't mean to rem-i-nisce.

You can sure-ly bet that I won't for-get, 'cause I have-n't yet. Good - bye!

Clementine

from *Ella Fitzgerald Sings the Duke Ellington Songbook – Verve VE2-2535*

By Billy Strayhorn

Crazy Rhythm

from *Ella Fitzgerald: In Budapest – Pablo 5308*
Words by Irving Caesar
Music by Joseph Meyer and Roger Wolfe Kahn

he has no ___ brow. Ain't ___ it a shame! And ___ you're to blame!

What's the use of Pro - hi - bi - tion? You pro - duce the

same con - di - tion. Cra - zy Rhy-thm, I've ___ gone cra -

zy too.

Scat:

We got rock, we got

roll, we want to try to sat - is - fy you, so ___ we like to

try to do the kind of song, __ you know, the songs __ you'd

Half-sung:

like to hear: Old songs, __ new songs, __ sad songs, __

blue songs, _ good songs, _ bad songs, _ true songs, _

new songs. _ Cra - zy Rhy - thm, here's the door - way; I'll go my way,

you go your _ way. Cra - zy Rhy - thm, from now on _ we're

through. _____ Here is where we have _ a show - down; _

_ I'll go high if you're the low _ down. Cra - zy Rhy - thm, it's good-bye _ to

Jazz Waltz (a bit slower)

you, you, you, you. When a

high - brow meets a low - brow walk - ing a - long _____

_ Broad - way, _____ soon a high - brow, he has

no brow. Ain't it a shame! And _____ you're to blame!

E and D Blues

from *Ella Fitzgerald: Daydream - The Best of the*
Duke Ellington Songbook – Verve/Polygram 5272232

Words and Music by Duke Ellington and John Sanders

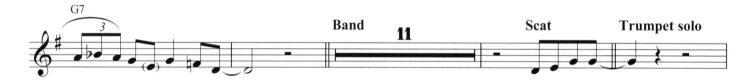

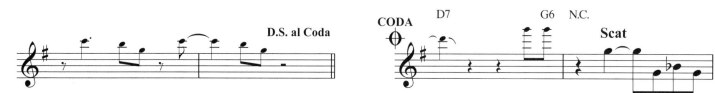

Dinah

from *Bing Crosby: 16 Most Requested Songs – Columbia/Legacy CK-48974*
Words by Sam M. Lewis and Joe Young
Music by Harry Akst

change her mind a - bout __ me. ____ Oh, _____

Di - nah, should you wan - der to Chi - na,

I would hop an o - cean lin - er just the be with Di - nah

Twice as fast

Tpt.:

Lee.

Backing Vocals:

(Di - nah, is there an - y - one
(Di - nah, with the Dix - ie eyes

fin - er ____ in the state of Car - o - li - na? ____
blaz - ing; ____ how I love to sit and gaze in -

1.

If there is and you know her, you know her, then show her to me.) __
- to the eyes of Di - nah

2.

Lee.) (My Di - nah, ev - 'ry night, why should I ____

shake with fright? __ Be - cause my Di - nah might __ change her mind __ a - bout

me.) _____ (Di - nah, if you wand - ered to

Chi - na, ___ I would hop an o - cean lin - er ___

Scat

just to be with Di - nah.)

Lead: Scat

Ev - 'ry night, _

why do I ___ shake with fright? 'Cause my Di - nah might

change her mind _ a - bout me. (The name of this song is

(Said it!)   (Snag it!)
Di - nah.   The name of this song is   Di - nah.   The name of this song is

(Ah,   tell it!)
Di - nah.   The name of this song is   Di - nah.)   Di - nah, _

_   she   wan - dered to Chi - na... _   The   state   of   Car - o - li -

- na...   If   there   is   and   you know her, I would like to have you show her to me.

Di - nah,   got those Dix - ie eyes   blaz - ing.   How I love to sit and

gaze   in -   to the eyes of Di - nah Lee.

Trumpet solo:
                                                 Ah, _____   Di - nah, _

should   you   wan - der to Chi - na,   would   get   me   an o - cean

lin - er   just   to be with Di - nah Lee. _

Dipsy Doodle

from *Ella Fitzgerald: The Early Years Pt. 1 – GRP 26182*

By Larry Clinton

The Dip-sy Doo-dle's a thing __ to be-ware; __ the Dip-sy Doo-dle will

get in your hair. __ And if it gets you, it could-n't be worse; __

the things you say will come out __ in re-verse. __ Like, "You love I and

me love you." __ That's the way the Dip-sy Doo-dle works. __

The Dip-sy Doo-dle is eas-y to find; __ it's al-most al-ways in the

back of your mind. __ You nev-er know it un-til it's too late, __

and then you're in such a ter - ri - ble state. _ Like,"The moon _ jumped _ o - ver the cow, _

_ hey did - dle." That's the way the Dip - sy Doo - dle works. _

When you think that you're cra - zy, you're the vic - tim of the Dip - sy Doo -

dle. But it's not _ your mind _ that's ha - zy, it's your tongue _

Scat

_ that's at fault, _ not your noo - dle. _____

(D)-dip dip dip

dip dip - sy doo - dle. You think you're cra - zy, the things _ that you say. _ Like,

Scat

That's the way the Dip - sy Doo - dle works. _

Trombone solo   **Band**

4   12   8   13

75

Ella Hums the Blues

from *Ella Fitzgerald: Songs from Pete Kelly's Blues* – Decca DL 8166

Words by Sammy Cahn
Music by Ray Heindorf

Slow Swing (♩ = 80)

Piano

Flying Home

from *Ella Fitzgerald: Gold – Verve B951102*

Music by Benny Goodman and Lionel Hampton

Lyric by Sid Robin

Mer - ri - ly we roll a - long on a

deep, deep, deep blue sea.

Hors - es, hors - es, hors - es!

Flat Foot Floogee

from *Slim Gaillard: Cement Mixer – Proper 1347*

Words and Music by Slim Gaillard, Slam Stewart and Bud Green

From This Moment On

from *Roberta Gambarini: So in Love – Emarcy 1796010*

Words and Music by Cole Porter

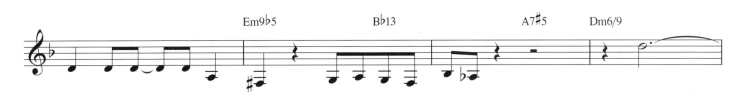

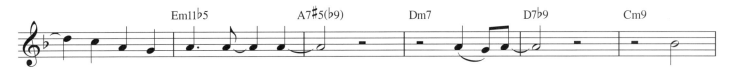

Eb7#5(#9)   D7#5(#9)   G13   C7#5(b9)

F6/9   A7#5(b9) Dm6/9   N.C.

Drum Solo   **Vocal**
                              Dm6/9   Em11b5   A7#5(#9)

28

From   this   mo - ment   on,

D(addb6)   Dm9 Dm6/9 Cm9   F13b5(b9)   Bbmaj9   Eb13#11

you   for   me,   dear; ___   on - ly ___ two   for   tea, ___

Gee Baby, Ain't I Good to You

from *Karrin Allyson: Azure-Té – Concord 4641*

Words by Don Redman and Andy Razaf
Music by Don Redman

Slow bluesy feel (♩ = 66)

Bass Solo

Love __ makes me treat you the way __ that I do; gee ba - by, ain't I good to you. __ Noth-in' too good for a boy so good and true. Gee ____ ba-by, ain't I ____ good to you. __ I bought you that coat for Christ - mas; a dia - mond ring. __ I bought you that Ca-dil-lac car, my ba - by; I went and bought you ev - 'ry - thing. Love makes me treat you __ the way __ that I do. Gee ____ ba-by, ain't I good to you. __

Violin Solo

Scat

Bass Solo

Scat

Heebie Jeebies

from *Louis Armstrong: The Best of the Hot Five and Hot Seven Recordings – Sony 5055*
By Boyd Atkins

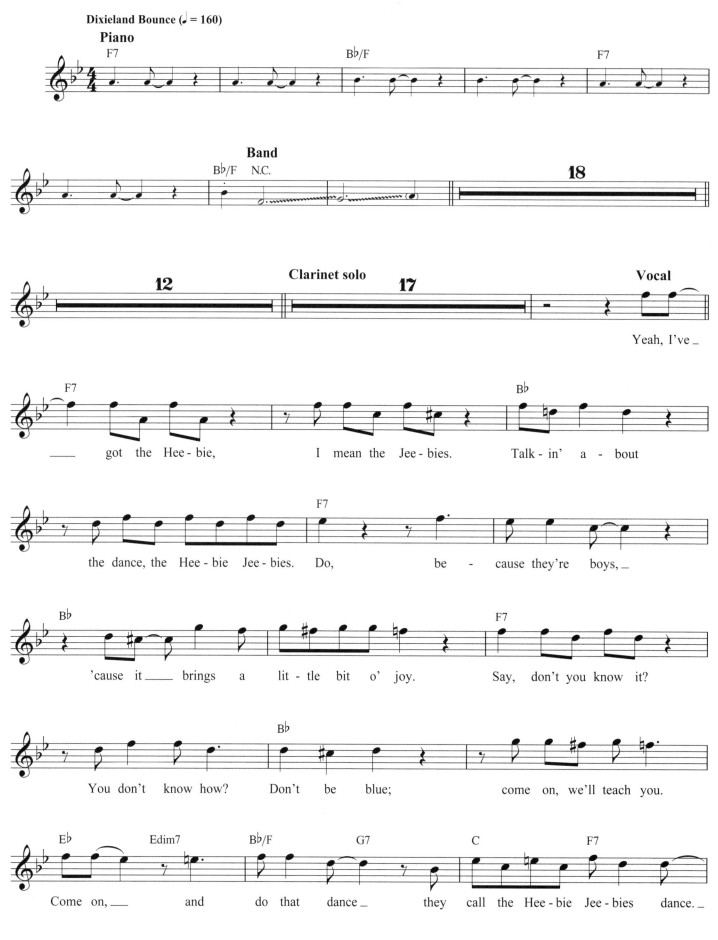

Yes ma'am, __ pa-pa's got the Hee-bie Jee-bies __ dance. Yeah,

Scat

So

come on now __ and do that dance _ they call the Hee-bie Jee-bies dance.

Sweet ma - ma, pa-pa got to do the Hee-bie Jee-bies dance. ____

Band

Whoo! got the Hee-bie Jee-bies. What-cha

do - in' with the Hee-bies? I just have _

___ to have the Hee-bies!

Honeysuckle Rose

from *Eddie Jefferson: The Jazz Singer – Evidence 22062*

Words by Andy Razaf
Music by Thomas "Fats" Waller

Hey, ___ it was hon - ey - suck - le rose... ___

Don - nie, blow! _

Trumpet solo

Hey, hey,— hey, hey,—

—— it's hon - ey - suck - le rose!

How High the Moon

from *Ann Hampton Callaway: To Ella with Love – Sindrome 71577689332*

Lyrics by Nancy Hamilton
Music by Morgan Lewis

Honeysuckle Rose

from *Roy Eldridge and Mel Tormé:*
1947 WNEW Saturday Night Swing Session – Everest FS 231
Words by Andy Razaf
Music by Thomas "Fats" Waller

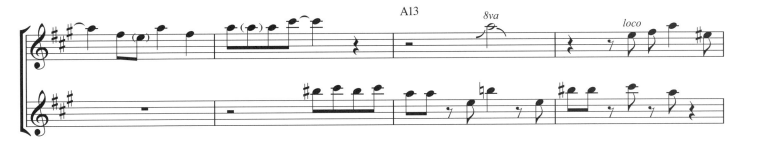

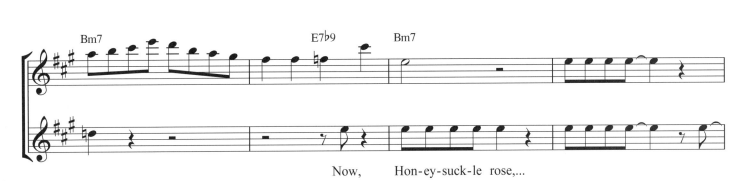

Now,　　Hon-ey-suck-le rose,...

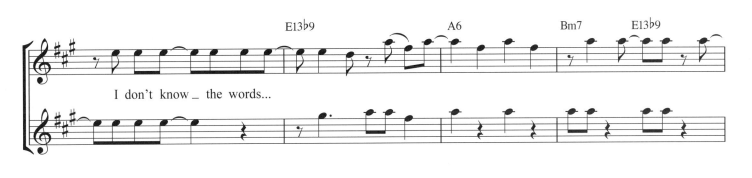

I don't know — the words...

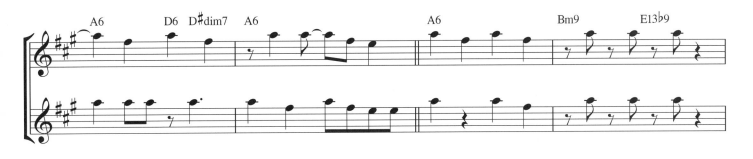

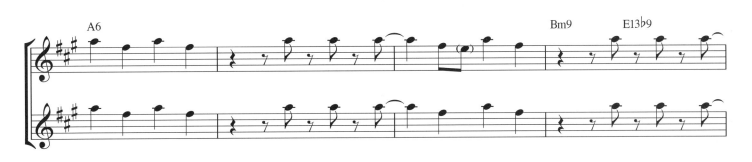

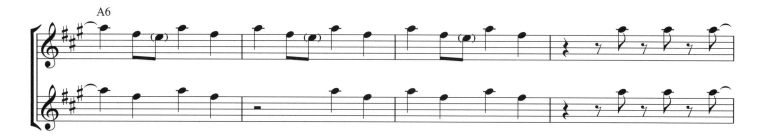

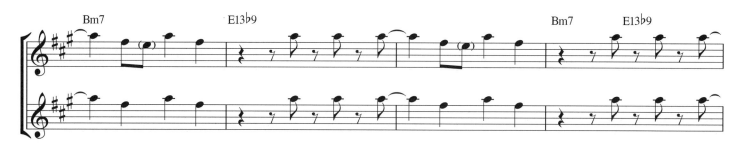

Sax Solo

Scat

(Sax Solo continues)

Scat

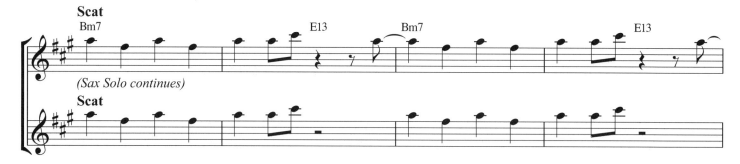

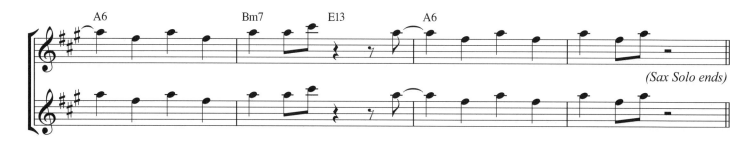

(Sax Solo ends)

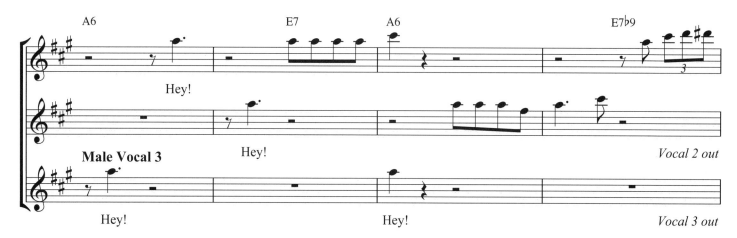

Hey!

Hey!

Male Vocal 3

Hey!

Vocal 2 out

Hey!

Hey!

Vocal 3 out

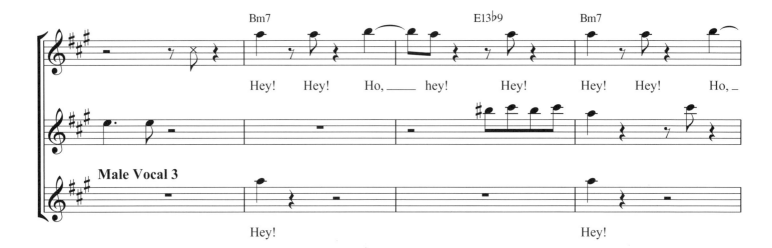

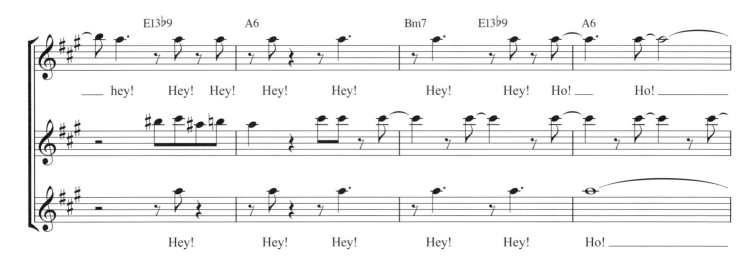

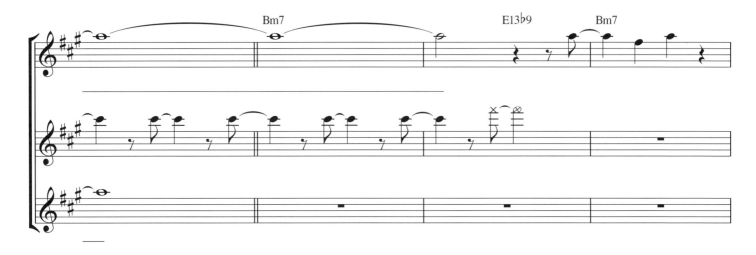

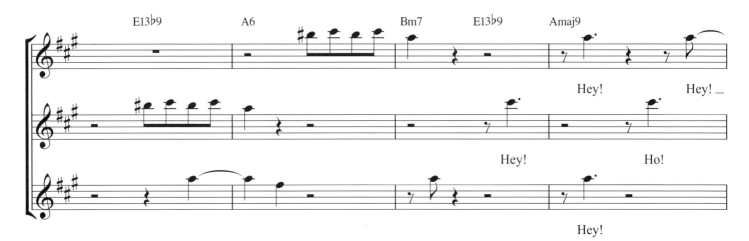

Ho!   Ho!

Hey!   *Vocal 3 out*

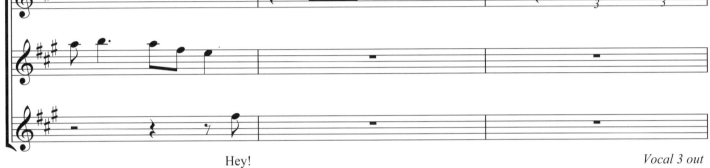

How High the Moon

from *Ella Fitzgerald: Lullabies of Birdland – Verve 1724765*

Lyrics by Nancy Hamilton
Music by Morgan Lewis

Though the words _ may be wrong to this song, ___ we hope _ you liked high, _

_____ high, ___ high, ___ high, high ___ is the moon! _____

I Ain't Got Nothin' But the Blues

from *Karrin Allyson: Daydream – Concord 4773*

Words by Don George
Music by Duke Ellington

G7   B♭/C

F7   B♭7   F7   E7♭9

Well, _____

A13

_____ the band   is   swing - in'; ___   the folks   are   sing-in'. ___

D13

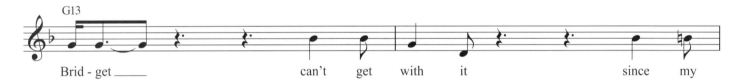

I   just can't seem ___   to   let ___ my   hair down. _____   Be-lieve me,

G13

Brid - get _____   can't   get   with   it   since   my

B♭maj7/C   Cdim7   B♭/C

ev - er   lov - in'   ba - by   left town.   Ain't got   no   rest   in   my

F7

slum - ber. _____   Ain't got   no   win - nin's   to ___

Dm7   G7

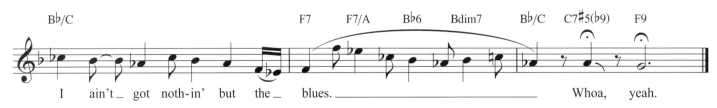

lose. _____   Ain't got   no   tel - e - phone ___ num-bers;

B♭/C   F7   F7/A   B♭6   Bdim7   B♭/C   C7♯5(♭9)   F9

I   ain't ___ got noth-in' but the ___ blues. _____   Whoa,   yeah.

I Got Rhythm

from *Sheila Jordan: I've Grown Accustomed to the Bass – High Note 7042*

Music and Lyrics by George Gershwin and Ira Gershwin

Bass Solo **95**

Vocal

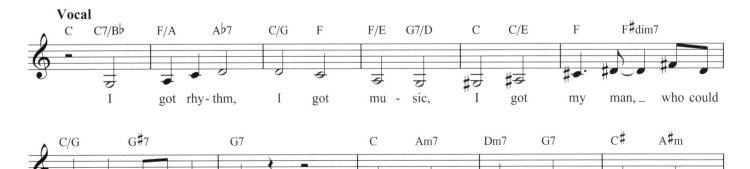

I got rhy-thm, I got mu-sic, I got my man,_ who could

ask for an-y-thing more? I got dai-sies in green

I Can't Give You Anything But Love

from *Sarah Vaughan: Capitol Sings Jimmy McHugh – Capitol/EMI 32565*

Words and Music by Jimmy McHugh and Dorothy Fields

Scat

Vibraphone Solo

Band   **Vocal**

Gee, I'd like to see ya,

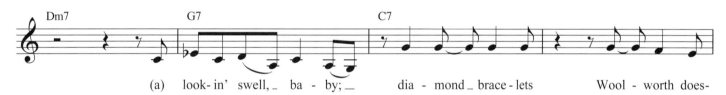

(a) look-in' swell, _ ba - by; _ dia - mond _ brace - lets   Wool - worth does-

n't sell, _____ (a) ba - by. _ Till that _ luck - y   day, you know darn _

_ well, _____ ba - by, _____ I can't _ give you   an - y - thing, _

ain't gon - na give _ you _ an - y - thing, _   I can't give   you ____

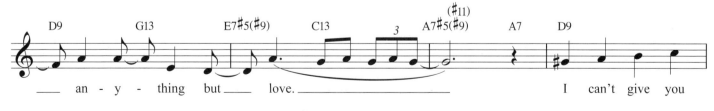

_ an - y - thing but _ love. _____   I can't give you

Band

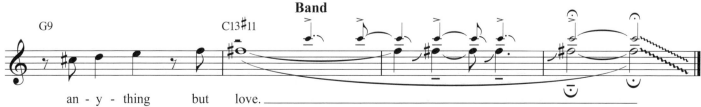

an - y - thing   but   love. _____

I'm in the Mood for Love

from *King Pleasure: Moody's Mood for Love – Collectables 5197*

Words and Music by Jimmy McHugh and Dorothy Fields

in your eyes, ___ bright as stars ___ that shine ___ up a - bove you

in the clear blue skies? ___ How I wor-ry 'bout you. Just can't live my life with-out you. Ba-by, come here, ___ don't

have no fear. Oh, is there a won-der why ___ I'm real - ly feel - ing in the

mood ___ for love? So tell me, why _____ start to think a - bout this

weath - er, my dear? This ___ lit - tle dream might fade a - way. There I

go, ___ talk-ing out of my head a-gain. Oh ba-by, won't you come and put our two hearts to-geth-er? ___

That would make me strong ___ and real. ___ Ooh, ___ when we are one, I'm not a -

fraid, _____ I'm not a - fraid! If there's a cloud up a - bove us, _____ go

on and let it rain; I'm sure our love to-geth-er will en - dure a hur - ri - cane. Oh my ba-by,

It's Not for Me to Say

from *Tania Maria: The Beat of Brazil – View Video 72034*

Words by Al Stillman
Music by Robert Allen

Per - haps, ___ the glow of ___ love will grow ___ with ___

___ ev -'ry pass-ing day, ___ or we may nev - er meet a - gain; ___

___ but then, _____ it's not for me to ___ say. ___

Scat

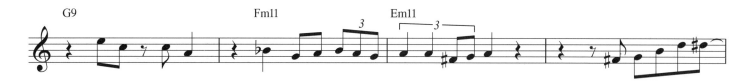

It's not for me to say ____

you love me. ____

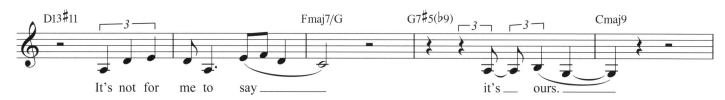

It's not for me to say _____ it's ___ ours. ____

Ca - ro, _____ but dear, __ for the mo-ment,

I can hold you fast,

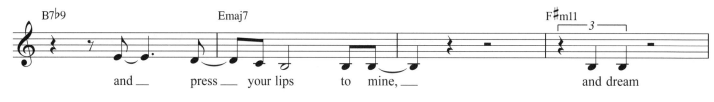

and __ press __ your lips to mine, __ and dream

that love __ will last. ____

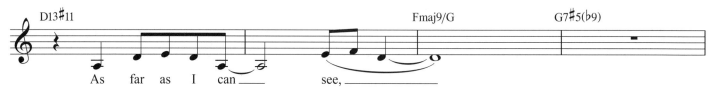

As far as I can __ see, _____

128

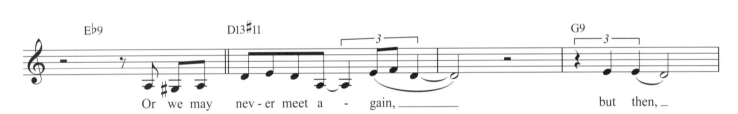

Or we may nev- er meet a - gain, _____ but then, _

it's not for me to _____ say. _____

We may nev- er meet a - gain, _____ but then, _

it's not for me to say. _____

But then, ___ it's not for me to say. _____ Mm, _____

oh, _____ yeah yeah yeah. Or we may nev-er meet a-gain, _____

Scat

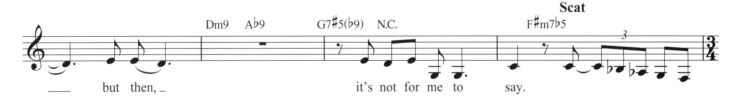

___ but then, _ it's not for me to say.

It Don't Mean a Thing

(If It Ain't Got That Swing)

from *Ella Fitzgerald Sings the Duke Ellington Songbook – Verve VE2-2535*

Words and Music by Duke Ellington and Irving Mills

It's All Right with Me

from *Connie Evingson: Stockholm Sweetnin' – Minnehaha Music 2007*

Words and Music by Cole Porter

It's the wrong time, _____ and _ the wrong _ place. Though your

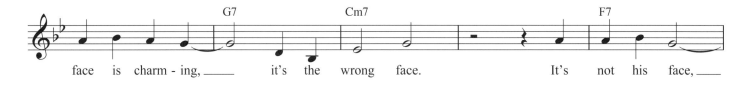

face is charm - ing, _____ it's the wrong face. It's not his face, _____

____ but such a charm - ing ___ face, _____ that it's all ___ right _____ with

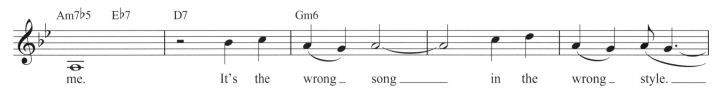

me. It's the wrong _ song _____ in the wrong _ style. _____

Ja-Da

from *Leo Watson: Anthology of Scat Singing, Vol. 3 – Masters of Jazz 803*

Words and Music by Bob Carleton

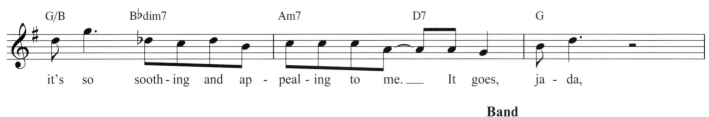

it's so sooth-ing and ap-peal-ing to me. __ It goes, ja - da,

Band

ja - da, ja - da ja - da jing jing jing. __

Scat

Scat

Band continues...

Clarinet solo

16

Scat

Jin - gle bells, jin - gle bells, jin - gle all the way!

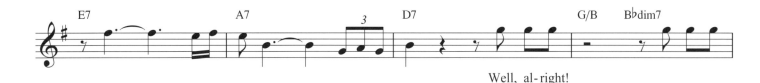

Well, al-right!

Trumpet solo

Scat

16

Ja - da, _____ ja - da, _____

ja - da ja - da jing jing jing. _____

Jumpin' at the Woodside

from *Jon Hendricks and Friends: Freddie Freeloader – Sony 53487*

Music by Count Basie
Words by Jon Hendricks

I got-ta go, ____ (Jump, jump,

____ jump, jump! I wan-na blow, ____ Jump, jump, jump, jump! I got-ta go. ____ Jump, jump,

jump, jump! I got-ta groove, I wan-na move, I got-ta have it, ba-by, groove. I got-ta
Jump, jump, jump, jump!)

jump, jump!) Not ____ in my i-mag-i-na-tion; ain't no mo-tel, __ I'll

tell you where the place is. Bet-cha nev-er heard of such a groov-y ho-tel.

Cop a move and then you'll bling-a-ding-a-ding. I got-ta split, ____ (Jump, jump,

____ jump, jump! I got-ta go, ____ Jump, jump, jump, jump! I wan-na blow. ____ Jump, jump,

mean,   they're jump - in' *Vocal ad lib.*   just have to

Dm7   **Dm7/G**   **C6**

know what you can do,   shake it,   blow it out.   *Vocal ad lib.*

Dm7   **Dm7/G**

Ev - 'ry bod - y has a ball at my ho - tel.

C6   **C7**

What a sto - ry I could tell!   I fin - ish up a gig, and might

                            F6

nev - er wig, you nev - er have to wor - ry, oh no, to find a place to get it, got it real - ly

D7   **G7**

go - in' on. ____   You can dig it, and you'll have a ball at home.

C6

Dig it!   you'll flip ____ it,   swell!   I ____ dig the Wood - side,

                            Dm7   **Dm7/G**

man, that's where I'm go - in'.   I been a lit - tle wool - y, 'cause I

Scat

C6   **Dm7**   **G7**   **C6**

real - ly have a ball at my ho - tel, you know.

30

Female Vocal   **Male Vocal**

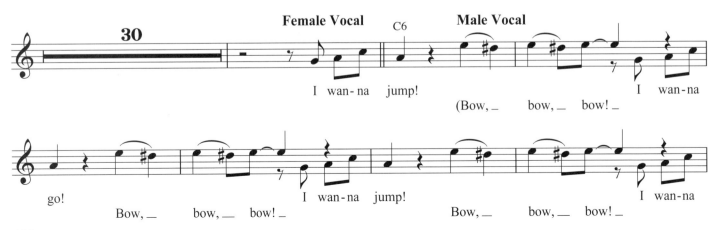

I wan-na   jump!   I wan-na
(Bow, __   bow, __   bow! __

go!   I wan-na   jump!   I wan-na
Bow, __   bow, __   bow! __   Bow, __   bow, __   bow! __

Male Vocal

jump! I wan-na go! I wan-na jump! I wan-na go! We're go-in' jump-in'. We're gon-na
Bow!) _____ *(Other vocals continue vamping)*

change you up. C-'mon, jump in, and I'm-a nev-er gon-na stop. You got-ta

Female Vocal

jump in... *Vocal ad lib.* you can jump at the Wood-side, yeah. Now,
Ooh

Dm7

wee! _____
(Other vocals continue vamping)

Dm7/G   C6

Won't you have a good time... We'll have such a good time... *Vocal ad lib.*

Dm7   Dm7/G

C6

Yeah, ___ *(ad lib.)* Just do it more. Yeah, just do it more.

Dm7   Dm7/G   C6

Yeah, just do it more. Yeah, just do it more... *Vocal ad lib.*

Dm7

Slow Swing feel

Dm7/G   N.C.   C7/E   F A♭/G♭   G   C6
rall.

Yes, ___ we're jump-in' ___ at the ___ Wood - side!

147

Just Friends

from *Mel Tormé: Rob McConnell and the Boss Brass – Concord CCD 4306*

Lyrics by Sam M. Lewis
Music by John Klenner

Scat (tutti w/ band)

died. The sto-ry ends; ___ we're ___ just friends.

Band

Trombone Solo

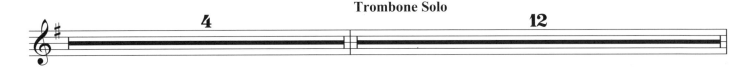

Scat

Trombone Solo   **Scat**

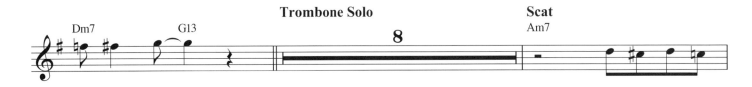

Trombone Solo

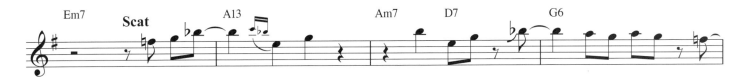

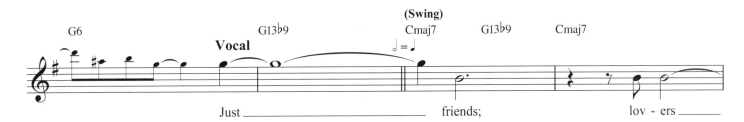

Just _____ friends;   lov - ers _____

____ no ___ more. __   Just _____ friends, ___   but not the ___ same as be-

fore.   Just   to   think   what   we   have   been ___   and

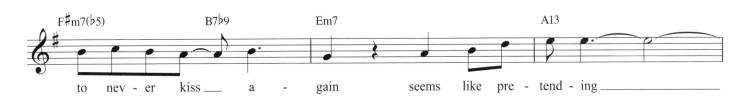

to nev - er kiss ___ a - gain   seems   like pre - tend - ing _____

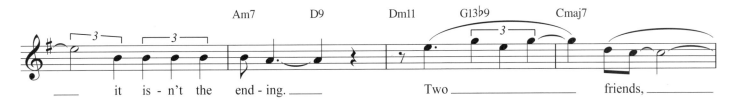

____ it is - n't the end - ing. ___   Two _____ friends, _____

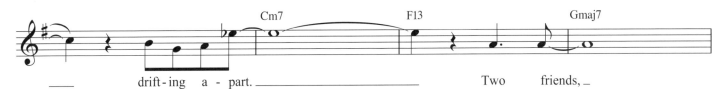

____ drift - ing a - part. _____   Two   friends, __

with one ___ bro - ken ___ heart. ___ We ___ lived, ___ laughed, ___ and cried, ___ and _____ sud-den - ly ___ love died. ___ The sto - ry ends, _____ the ___ sto - ry ___ ends, _____ the ___ sto - ry ___ ends, ___ the the the the sto - ry ends, _____ the sto - ry ___ ends, ___ the sto-no - no - no - no - no - ry - ry ends, _____ the sto - ry ends, _____ and we're just...

(Tempo I)

Scat

Just You, Just Me

from *Ella Fitzgerald: Ella Swings Lightly – Verve/GRP/Polygram 5175352*

Music by Jesse Greer
Lyrics by Raymond Klages

Just You, Just Me

from *Tierney Sutton: Blue in Green – Telarc 83522*

Music by Jesse Greer
Lyrics by Raymond Klages

let's find a co-zy spot to cud-dle and coo.

Scat   **Scat**

Just us, just me.

I've missed an aw-ful lot; my trou-ble is you.

Oh gee, what are your charms for?

What are my arms for? Use your i-mag-i-na-tion. Just

you, just me. I'll tie a lov-ers' knot

Scat

'round won-der-ful you.

3

Line for Lyons

from *Fay Claassen Sings Two Portraits of Chet Baker – Jazz N' Pulz 497*

By Gerry Mulligan

Scat

Line for Lyons

from *Karrin Allyson: I Didn't Know About You – Concord Jazz 4543*

By Gerry Mulligan

Lover, Come Back to Me

from *Roberta Gambarini: Easy to Love – New Forward Music Inc. 1122*
Lyrics by Oscar Hammerstein II
Music by Sigmund Romberg

love is old. ___ And as I'm wait-ing here, ___ this heart of mine ___ keeps ___

___ cry - ing, "Lov - er come ___ back ___ to me." ___

Scat

Piano Solo

Scat

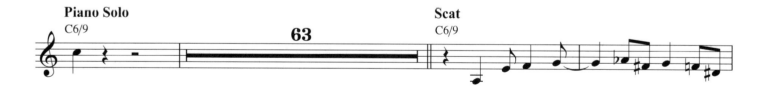

Drum Solo   **Piano Solo**   **Drum Solo**

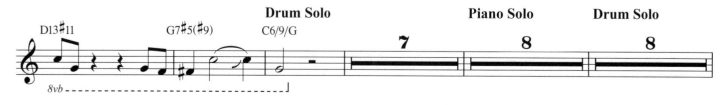

Lover, Come Back to Me

from *Anita O'Day: Collates – Universal 9120*

Lyrics by Oscar Hammerstein II
Music by Sigmund Romberg

The sky was blue, and high a-bove.

The moon was new, and so was love.

This ea-ger heart of mine was sing - ing, "Lov-er, where can you be?"

You came at last, love had its day.

That day has passed, you've gone a - way.

Ea - ger heart of mine is sing - ing, "Lov - er, come

back to me." I re-mem-ber ev - 'ry lit-tle thing

you used to do; I'm so lone - ly.

re - mem - ber ev - 'ry lit - tle thing ___ you used to do;

I'm so ___ lone - ly. Ev - 'ry road I walk _

___ a - long I walked a - long with you no ___ won - der ___

___ I'm ___ so lone - ly. The sky ___ is blue,

and high ___ a - bove; the moon ___ is new, and so is

love. ___ And while ___ I'm wait - ing here, _ this heart of mine _ is sing-

- ing, ___ "Lov - er come back to me; ___

lov - er come back ___ to ___ me." ___

Lullaby of Birdland

from *Ann Hampton Callaway: To Ella with Love – Sindrome 71577689332*

Words by George David Weiss
Music by George Shearing

Lullaby of Birdland

from *Dianne Reeves: Best of – Blue Note 5358672*

Words by George David Weiss
Music by George Shearing

Scat

Band   **Scat**

Vocal

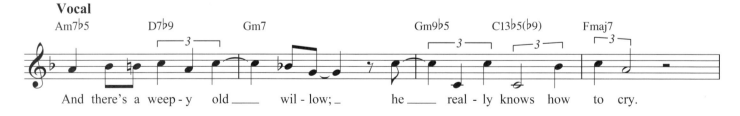

And there's a weep-y old ____ wil - low; _ he ____ real - ly knows how to cry.

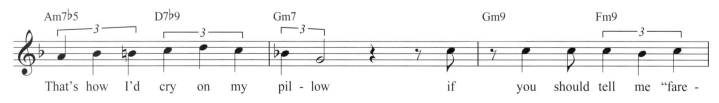

That's how I'd cry on my pil - low   if   you should tell me "fare-

Lullaby of Birdland

from *Mel Tormé: Lulu's Back in Town – Giants of Jazz 53010*

Words by George David Weiss
Music by George Shearing

fly-ing off to Bird-land, high __ in the sky __ up a - bove,   just be - cause we're in   love. __

Scat

Trumpet Solo   **Scat**

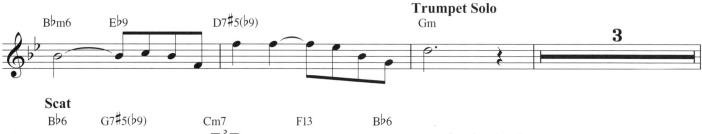

Trumpet Solo

Scat

Trumpet Solo **Scat**

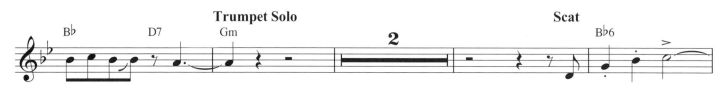

Trumpet Solo **Scat**

Trombone Solo

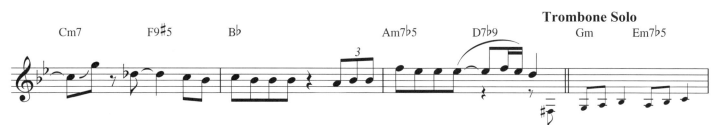

Scat

Trombone Solo

Scat

Trombone Solo

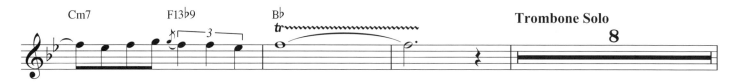

Scat

Lullaby of Birdland

from *Sarah Vaughan's Golden Hits – Mercury/Universal Classics & Jazz 8248912*

Words by George David Weiss
Music by George Shearing

Oh, Lady Be Good!

from *Ann Hampton Callaway: To Ella with Love – Sindrome 71577689332*

Music and Lyrics by George Gershwin and Ira Gershwin

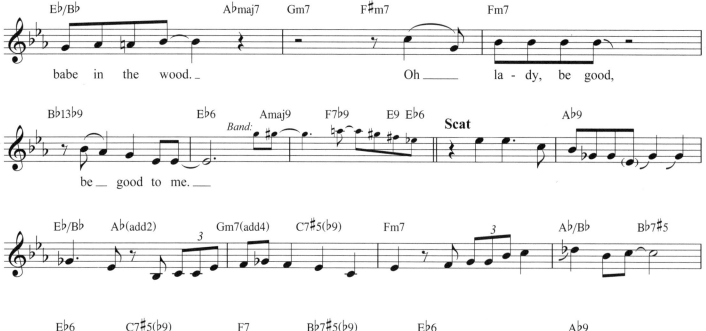

babe in the wood.

Oh _____ la - dy, be good,

be _ good to me. _____

Scat

Band **14**

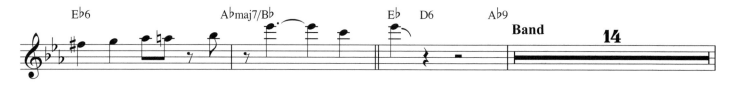

Mas Que Nada

from *Ella Fitzgerald: Things Ain't What They Used to Be – Reprise 2-26023*
Words and Music by Jorge Ben

na - da. Hey, ___ *mas ___ que na - da.*

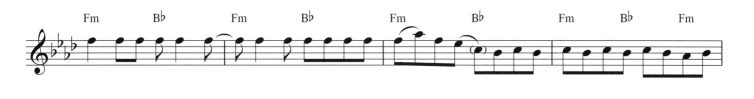

Begin fadeout

Nature Boy

from Kurt Elling: The Messenger – Blue Note 8527272

Words and Music by Eden Ahbez

Piano Solo **Scat**

Vocal

There

Oh, Lady Be Good!

from *Dianne Reeves: We All Love Ella – Verve 8833*

Music and Lyrics by George Gershwin and Ira Gershwin

Oh, _____ please have some _
_ pit - ty; _ I'm _____ all _
_ a - lone _ in this _ big cit - y. I tell you, I'm _____ just a
lone - some _ babe _ in the _ wood, so _ la - dy,
be _ good _ to _ me. _____ Oh _ la - dy,
la - dy be good to _____ me. _ La - dy, _____
be good to me.

Old Devil Moon

from *Carmen McRae: The Bethlehem Years – Universal/Verve 652122*

Words by E.Y. "Yip" Harburg
Music by Burton Lane

eyes,   mm! _

Talk - in' 'bout your   eyes,   child.   Your

eyes. ___   (a) Them eyes, ___   yeah.

Eyes... ___   Them pret-ty eyes,   eye - eyes. _

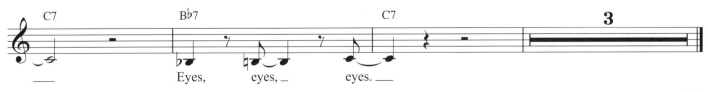

Eyes,   eyes, _   eyes. __

On the Sunny Side of the Street

from *Roberta Gambarini: Easy to Love – New Forward Music Inc. 1122*

Lyric by Dorothy Fields
Music by Jimmy McHugh

you'll _ sure - ly get what you need. _ Just di - rect _ your feet _

_ right up the sun - ny side of life, ___ the ver - y sun - ny...

Come on, come now! I know for sure there is a way to be on the sun - ny

side _ of life.

Scat

All that you have to do is lis - ten ___ to the sound that goes on to stay. _

___ Yes, it will nev - er ev - er fade _ a - way. ___

Come _ on   and just see what hap-pens. That   hap-py sound that's com-ing   on   is the sound of a

ten - or ___ sax - o - phone _   that is   played with heart and soul by Mis - ter

Son - ny   Stitt.   ...just to   be the sun-ny side. _

___   There _ it comes. ___   I love the sun, to

see my - self   but not nec-es-sar-ily know   it's Diz - zy.

Just ____

____ get your ___ kicks on _____ the side, the sun - ny side, the groov-y side, the ver-y side of the

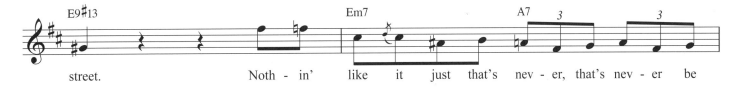

street. Noth - in' like it just that's nev - er, that's nev - er be

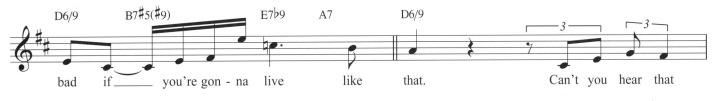

bad if_____ you're gon - na live like that. Can't you hear that

pit - ter, pat - ter, pit - ter pat - ter sound? _ For that pit - ter pat - ter sound is like a

tap - ping sound. Yes, ___ the sound of joy ___ lin - ger-ing on, o - ver and out. _

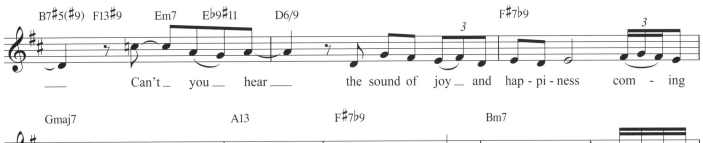

___ Can't _ you _ hear ___ the sound of joy _ and hap - pi - ness com - ing

o - ver? We're get-ting to the stars!

Head

208

Pick Yourself Up

from *Ann Hampton Callaway: Signature – Shanachie 5127*
Words by Dorothy Fields
Music by Jerome Kern

Mel would tip his hat to the hip-pest cat ___ who be-

gan im-prov-i-sa-tion that would lead to scat. ___ Where would Mel and

Scat

Lou-ie and El-la be ___ with-out ___ that feist - y fel-la?

Bass in unison -

St. Louis Blues

from *Ella Fitzgerald: Twelve Nights in Hollywood – Hip-O Select 2704402*

Words and Music by W.C. Handy

216

Lat - er! ___

Lat - er! _____

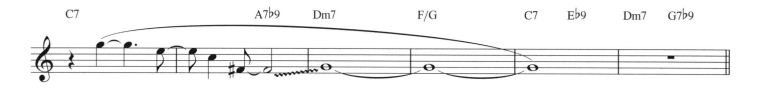

No, it don't mat - ter,

no it does-n't mat - ter, may not mat - ter.

Rockin' in Rhythm

from *Bunny Briggs: Charlie Barnet Dance Bash – Verve MGV2007*

By Duke Ellington, Irving Mills and Harry Carney

(a) Char-lie Bar - net. _____

Schulie A Bop

from *Sarah Vaughan's Finest Hour – Verve 5435972*

Words and Music by Sarah Vaughan and George Treadwell

I ain't mad at you, pret-ty ba-by;___ don't be mad at me.___

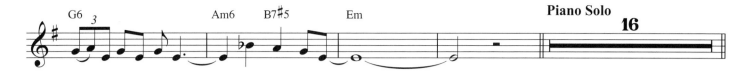

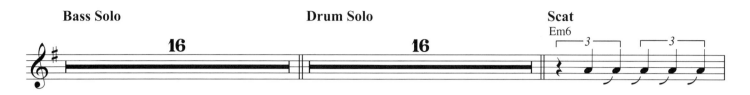

Shiny Stockings

from *Trish Hatley: I Remember – CD Baby/Kiss of Jazz 5637596077*

Words by Ella Fitzgerald
Music by Frank Foster

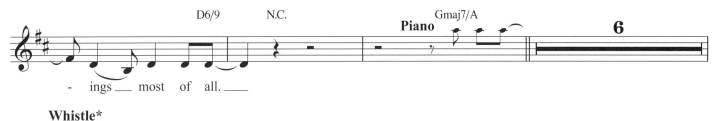

- ings ___ most of all. ___

Whistle*

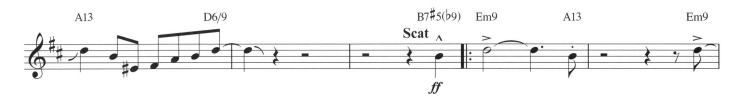

Whistle sounds 8va throughout.

Song for My Father

from Dee Dee Bridgewater: Love and Peace – Verve/Polygram 5274702

Words and Music by Horace Silver

love is real nice, _ but will dad ___ sac - ri - fice for ___ us too? _____ Let us

give him ___ his due. _____ We're ver - y proud to be ___

___ in his bi - o - graph-y. _____ We sing this song for him, _

and you. _____

Sing, Sing, Sing

from *Anita O'Day Sings the Winners – Verve AA8379392*

Words and Music by Louis Prima

sing, ____ sing, ____ sing! Ev - 'ry - bod - y start to sing. ____

Scat

Now ____ you're sing - in' ____

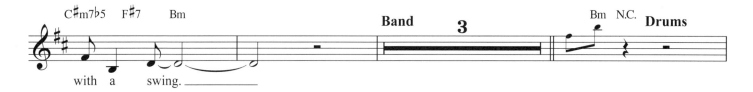

with a swing. ____

234

Some of These Days

from *Bing Crosby: Kraft Music Hall – JSP 6701*

Words and Music by Shelton Brooks

And __ you're gon-na be lone - ly __

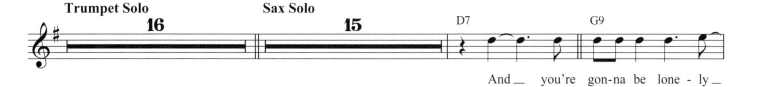

__ just for me on - ly, _____ 'cause you know, __ hon-ey, that you had your

way. And when you leave me, _____ you know _ it's gon-na grieve me.

You'll miss _ your lit-tle...

Squeeze Me

from *Roberta Gambarini: You Are There – Emarcy 1737067*

Words and Music by Clarence Williams and Thomas "Fats" Waller

Squeeze me, but don't you tease _____ me,

Piano Solo   **Scat**

yes.

Piano   **Scat**

Piano   **Scat**

Piano   **Scat**

Piano   **Scat**

Piano   **Vocal**

Oh, treat me sweet and gen - tle

when you hold _____ me tight. Just squeeze _____ me, but please don't

240

Stolen Moments

from *Mark Murphy: Stolen Moments – Muse MCD 5102*

Words and Music by Oliver Nelson

Scat Solo

Sto - len _____ mo - ments. _____ - ments. _____

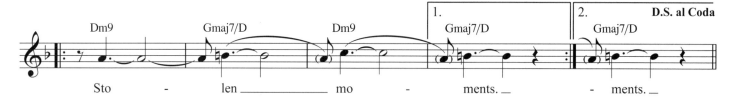

pan - to - mime! _____

(Voice: tacet to end)

There Will Never Be Another You

from *Ann Hampton Callaway: Bring Back Romance – DRG 91417*

Lyric by Mack Gordon
Music by Harry Warren

but they won't thrill me like ____ yours ____ used to ____ do. ____

____ I may dream a mil - lion dreams; ____ how can they come true ____

____ if there will nev - er ev - er be ____ an - oth - er you? Not you. ____

Piano Solo   **Bass Solo**   **Scat**

15   **16**

____

____ kiss, but they ____ won't thrill me like ____ yours ____ used ____ to do. ____

____ I ____ may dream a mil - lion dreams; ____ how can they come

There'll be ____ oth - er lips I'll ____

Suddenly In Walked Bud

from *Carmen McRae: Carmen Sings Monk – Sony 6619811*

Music by Thelonious Monk
Words by Jon Hendricks

Thou Swell

from *Meet Betty Carter and Ray Bryant – Epic 3202*
Words by Lorenz Hart
Music by Richard Rodgers

Piano Solo   **Scat**

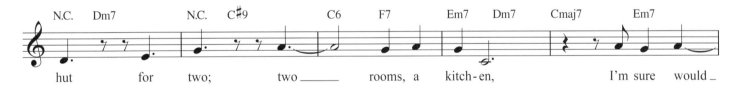

I'd   feel   so   rich   in ____ a

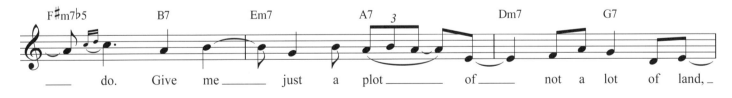

hut   for   two;   two ____ rooms, a   kitch-en,   I'm sure would _

____ do.   Give   me ____ just   a   plot ____ of ____ not a lot   of   land, _

____ and... _   **Scat**   Thou _

____ grand! _____

A-Tisket, A-Tasket

from *The Manhattan Transfer: Couldn't Be Hotter – Telarc 83586*

Words and Music by Ella Fitzgerald and Van Alexander

when she spied it on _____ the ground. _____ She took it, she

took it, my lit - tle yel - low bas - ket. And _____

if she does - n't bring it back, __ I think that I _____ will die. __

(Ba doo ba da da, ba

Scat solo

doo ba da da, ba doo ba da da, ba doo ba da da, ba doo ba da da.)

(A tis - ket, a tas - ket, I lost my yel-low bas -

Yeah, _____ and if that girl - lie don't ___ re - turn, ___ I
- ket.)

don't know what I'll do! _____ Oh dear, I

won - der won - der won - der where the bas - ket could ___ be! ___ (So do we!

So do we! So do we! So do we! So do we!)

Oh ___ gee, ___ you know, I...

(So do we! So do we! So do we!

So do we! So do we!) Oh,

West Coast Blues

from *Karrin Allyson: In Blue – Concord 2106CCJ*

Music by John L. (Wes) Montgomery
Lyrics by Sascha Burland

Yardbird Suite

from *Karrin Allyson: Azure-Té – Concord 4641*

By Charlie Parker

Bright Swing (♩ = 232)

Lyrics not included due to licensing restrictions.

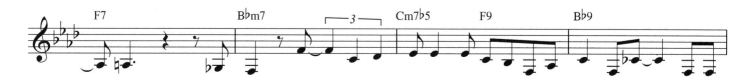

Sax Solo

Scat

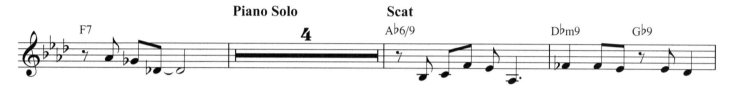

Yesterdays

from *Dianne Reeves: Dianne Reeves – Blue Note 46906*
Words by Otto Harbach
Music by Jerome Kern

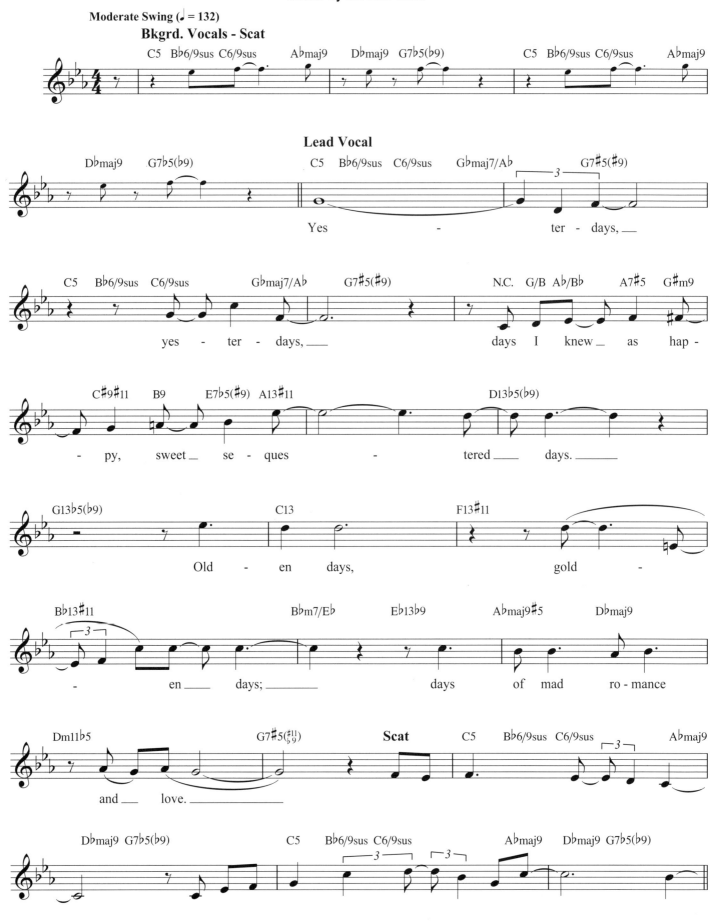

264

Begin fadeout

Zaz Zuh Zaz

from *Cab Calloway: On Film 1934-1950 – Flyright 944*

Words and Music by Cab Calloway and Harry A. White

When Smok-y Joe ___ came in-to town, ___ and he ___ kicked the gong ___ a-round, ___

an-y-place that he would go, ___ Min-nie the Mooch-er, she was sure _ to go, with her...

Scat

It makes no dif-f'rence where you go, _ there's _ one thing that they sure do know: ___

there's _ no need for them to be blue, ___ 'cause Zaz Zuh Zaz will al-ways _ see _ them through. _

Scat

Band

Freely
Scat

You'll Have to Swing It

from *Ella Fitzgerald: Pure Ella – Verve 539206*

Words and Music by Sam Coslow

and spring it! ___ And if you can't spring it, you'll sim-ply have to... ___

Fast Swing (♩ = 200)

Lis - ten, Pa - ga - ni - ni, please play ___ my rhap - so - dy. ___

___ And if you can-not play ___ it, won't ___ you ___ sing ___ it? ___

___ If the boys are bop - pin', ___ ain't no need in stop-

- pin'. ___

Lis - ten, Pa - ga - ni - ni, we breath-

- less - ly a - wait ___ your ___ mas - ter - ful ba - ton; come ___ on ___

and ___ spring ___ it. ___ If the boys are bop - pin', ___

ARTIST INDEX